Stink Fights, Earwax, and Other Marvelous Mammal Adaptations

LAURA PERDEW

Illustrated by Katie Mazeika

Can you haiku?

Mammal Adaptations

Stink fights and earwax,
Trunks, tunnels, and two-foot tongues,
Odd adaptations.

Not Lazy, Well-Adapted

Sloths just hang in trees,
As algae grows on their fur,
Green coat hiding them.

A Star-Nosed Mole

Fleshy tentacles
Form a star, touching, feeling,
Searching for dinner.

An Elephant's Trunk

That nose is part hose,
Snorkel, straw, fork, and alarm,
And, of course, sniffer.

Mammals have all kinds of marvelous adaptations to help them survive.

You might already know that giraffes have long necks to help them reach leaves on tall trees.

And that cheetahs are super fast, so they can catch a quick dinner.

But do you know how lemurs settle an argument?

Stink fights!

Ring-tailed lemurs produce a terrible scent. Sometimes, male lemurs rub this scent on their tails. Then, they wave their tails—and the smell—into the air. The lemur who can stand the stink the longest, wins!

By having a stink fight, male lemurs can settle things without getting hurt.

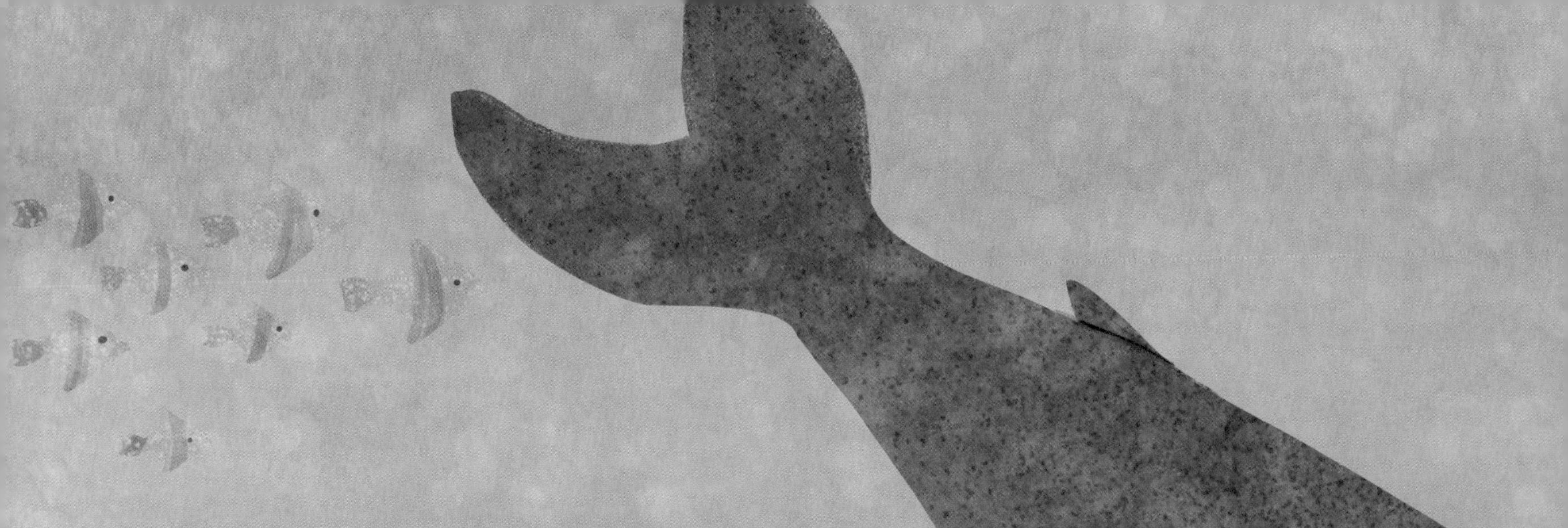

By studying whale earwax, scientists can learn the age of a whale.

Did you know that earwax is an adaptation, too?

It is! In some whales, wax builds up so much it creates a plug. Yup, no such thing as a whale Q-tip.

That's okay, though.

The earwax plug works like a hearing aid, helping whales to hear even better.

They also discover its life history and the health of its environment.

Elephants have an excellent sense of smell.

Like whales, you probably use your ears just for hearing. **Not African elephants!**

They use their huge ears for hearing

AND

for flapping to stay cool.

One of the best in the animal world!

They also stay cool by using their trunks like a hose to spray water over their backs.

Their trunks can be used as
a straw, **a snorkel**,
a fork, **fingers**, **an arm**,
and **an alarm**, too.

They even use it as a regular nose—**to sniff things!**

You know what else has
an impressive nose?

Star-nosed moles!

Their noses have 22 fleshy tentacles that form a star. But those noses aren't sniffing for food. They're feeling for food. Each tentacle is very sensitive and moves so fast the mole can identify its prey in less than half a second.

Try feeling around for a snack with your nose!

Star-nosed moles can touch up to 12 objects per second with their noses!

Since we're talking about noses,
take a look at the giant anteater.
It has a long, pointed snout.

Guess what's inside that long nose?

A 2-foot-long tongue!

Giant anteaters' tongues are like 2-foot-long strands of spaghetti . . .

. . . covered in sticky spit!

The **looooooong** snout and **looooooong** tongue are perfect for getting into a termite mound or anthill.

Can you imagine slurping up 30,000 insects a day with a tongue like that? Giant anteaters don't even chew—no teeth.

They just swallow. Yum?

Some types of bats
feast on insects, too.
You know what else they do?

Roost upside down!

They do this because they are too heavy to fly right up into the air like a bird. When they want to fly, they just let go.

How would you like to sleep upside down to make it easier to get out of bed?

Bats are the ONLY mammal that can fly.

Another unusual mammal is **the platypus!**

Take a look—they seem to be part **otter**,
beaver, and
duck.

Platypuses are also one of only a few venomous mammals. The males have sharp spurs on both ankles. Those spurs carry venom that can be deadly to anyone who dares to mess with them.

So don't make a platypus mad!

When the first platypus specimen was brought to Britain from Australia in the late 1700s, people thought it was a joke!

Pangolins and hedgehogs don't have venom or spurs, but they still have protection.

They wear suits of armor all the time.

While most mammals are covered in fur, pangolins are covered in scales. Hedgehogs are covered in quills.

What predator would want a mouthful of scales or quills?

Most don't!

Pangolins and hedgehogs roll into tight balls when threatened. This protects their soft underbellies, which don't have scales or quills.

Pangolins can even roll away from danger!

What about the poor naked mole rat?

They don't have any scales, quills, or fur. **They're, well, naked!**

Believe it or not, this is a great adaptation for staying cool in the hot East African desert. If they get cold, they cuddle!

They stay safe by living underground.

In fact, naked mole rats spend their entire lives underground. The network of tunnels includes rooms, just like you have in your house.

Beavers also build homes to keep them safe. **Have you ever heard the phrase, “busy as a beaver”?**

It’s because beavers spend A LOT of time building their lodges. They use sticks and reeds to make their lodge and seal it with mud. They even put in a chimney for air!

The best part is
the secret door—the
only way into the lodge is under water.

Beavers create dams in waterways, which form ponds.
Then, they build their lodges in the middle of the ponds, which also serve as important habitats for many kinds of plants and animals.

Sloths stay hidden in a different way.
For one thing, they don't move much.

And when they do move, they move very . . .

very . . .

slowly.

Sloths usually only go to the ground to poop!

In fact, they move so little that algae grow on their fur.

Ick?

Not for the sloth.

With green fur, they are camouflaged in the jungle, so they are hard to see. They're not lazy—they're well adapted!

Like sloths, southern elephant seals may look like a bunch of large, lazy bums—with funny noses—when they are on shore.

In the water, though, they move like **torpedoes.**

That's because of their body shape and powerful flippers. A seal can take a breath and make it last for up to two hours!

What would you do if you could swim like that?

Southern elephant seals can dive more than a mile looking for food such as fish and squid.

Camels are well adapted to living in a completely opposite environment—the **hot desert**.

Did you know that their humps are filled with fat, not water? The fat is like having an energy bar stuck on your back to use when you can't find food or water.

That's not all!

If you see a camel with a drooping hump, you'll know that the camel has used up the stored fat.

Camels also have two rows of long eyelashes to keep sand out of their eyes.

And, they can close their nostrils.

Go ahead, you try it!

Every mammal,

including you,

has marvelous adaptations that help it survive!

What are some others that you know?

Activity Time!

How are HUMANS Adapted?

Humans are mammals, too. And we live in many different ecosystems on earth: deserts, tropical rainforests, arctic regions, mountains, and grasslands.

WHAT YOU NEED

paper, colored pencils or crayons

WHAT YOU DO

Think about how people might be adapted to living in different places.
What do they wear?
How do they move around?
What do their homes look like?
What kinds of food do they eat?

Draw a person (or a family) from one place.
What kinds of clothes are they wearing?
How do the kids get to school?
What do they eat for dinner?
Their adaptations will depend on the weather and the environment where they live.

Now, try drawing someone from another ecosystem.
How are they the same as the others? How are they different?

Glossary

Giant anteater

adaptation: something about a plant or animal that helps it survive in its habitat.

algae: a simple living thing found in water that is like a plant but without roots, stems, or leaves.

armor: a covering that protects the body in battle.

camouflage: colors or patterns that animals use to blend in with their environments.

climate: the average weather patterns in an area during a long period of time.

ecosystem: a community of living and nonliving things and their environments.

environment: the area in which something lives.

habitat: an area that a plant or animal calls home.

haiku: a short, simple poem that usually has 17 syllables.

hibernate: to sleep through the winter.

Pink fairy armadillo

credit: Attis1979 (CC BY 2.0)

mammal: a type of animal, such as a human, dog, or cat. Mammals are born live, feed milk to their young, and usually have hair or fur covering most of their skin.

predator: an animal that hunts another animal for food.

prey: an animal that is hunted and eaten by another animal.

roost: a place where birds or bats settle to rest.

snorkel: a short, curved tube that a swimmer can breathe through while under water.

species: a group of living things that are closely related and produce young.

specimen: a sample of something, such as a plant or animal.

Platypus

credit: Feeding Platypus, Brisbane City Council (CC BY 2.0)

tentacle: a slender, flexible limb on an animal.

torpedo: an oval-shaped underwater missile.

warm-blooded: describes animals that can keep themselves warm with their own body heat, such as humans, birds, and bears.

venomous: poisonous.

CHECK OUT THE OTHER TITLES IN THIS SET!

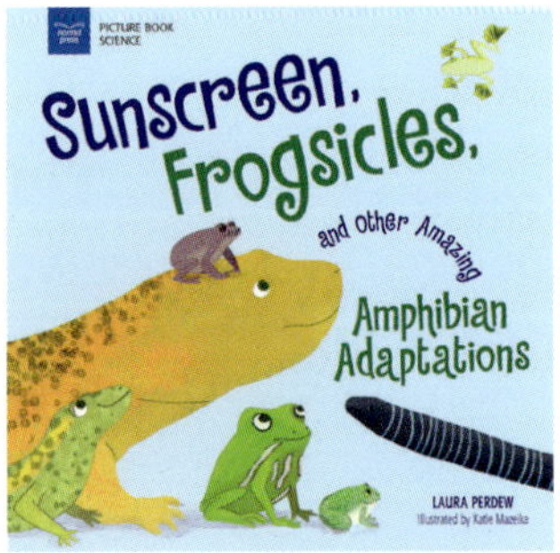

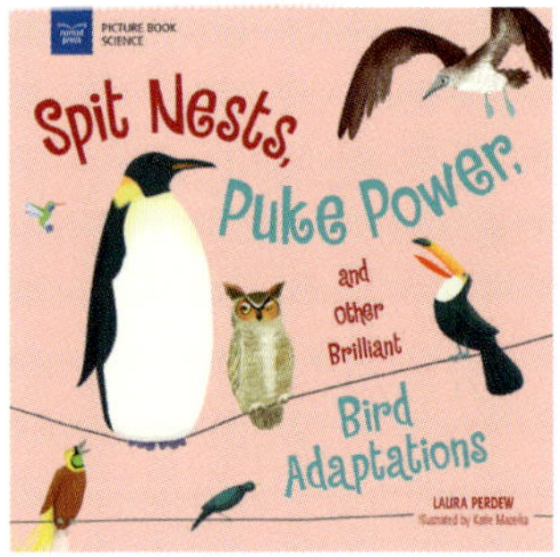

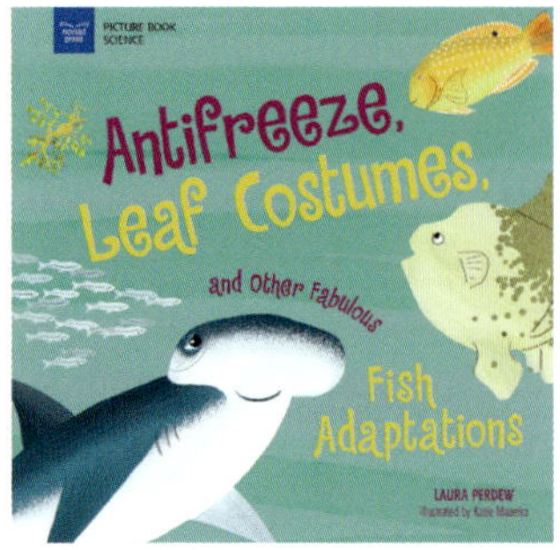

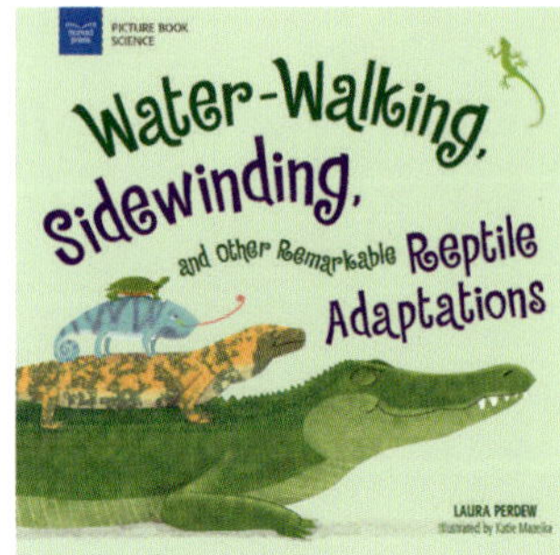

Nomad Press

A division of Nomad Communications

10 9 8 7 6 5 4

ISBN Softcover: 978-1-61930-960-9
ISBN Hardcover: 978-1-61930-957-9

Educational Consultant, Marla Conn

Questions regarding the ordering of this book should be addressed to
Nomad Press
PO Box 1036, Norwich, VT 05055
www.nomadpress.net

Printed in the United States.